THE NUTCRACKER
FOR CLASSICAL PLAYERS

To access recorded piano accompaniments online, visit:
www.halleonard.com/mylibrary

Enter Code
1319-6796-1403-2968

ISBN: 978-1-5400-9708-8

HAL•LEONARD®

Visit Hal Leonard Online at
www.halleonard.com

Contact us:
Hal Leonard
7777 West Bluemound Road
Milwaukee, WI 53213
Email: info@halleonard.com

In Europe, contact:
Hal Leonard Europe Limited
42 Wigmore Street
Marylebone, London, W1U 2RN
Email: info@halleonardeurope.com

In Australia, contact:
Hal Leonard Australia Pty. Ltd.
4 Lentara Court
Cheltenham, Victoria, 3192 Australia
Email: info@halleonard.com.au

HOW TO USE HAL LEONARD ONLINE AUDIO

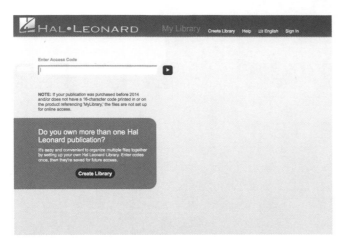

Because of the changing use of media, and the fact that fewer people are using CDs, we have made a shift to companion audio accessible online. In many cases, rather than a book with CD, we now have a book with an access code for online audio, including performances, accompaniments or diction lessons. Each copy of each book has a unique access code. We call this Hal Leonard created system "My Library." It's simple to use.

Go to www.halleonard.com/mylibrary and enter the unique access code found on page one of a relevant book/audio package.

The audio tracks can be streamed or downloaded. If you download the tracks on your computer, you can add the files to a CD or to your digital music library, and use them anywhere without being online. See below for comments about Apple and Android mobile devices.

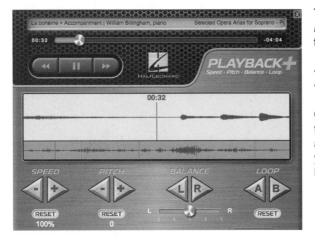

There are some great benefits to the My Library system. *Playback+* is exclusive to Hal Leonard, and when connected to the Internet with this multi-functional audio player you can:

• Change tempo without changing pitch
• Transpose to any key

Optionally, you can create a My Library account, and store all the companion audio you have purchased there. Access your account online at any time, from any device, by logging into your account at www.halleonard.com/mylibrary. Technical help may be found at www.halleonard.com/mylibrary/help/

Apple/iOS

Question: On my iPad and iPhone, the Download links just open another browser tab and play the track. How come this doesn't really download?

Answer: The Safari iOS browser will not allow you to download audio files directly in iTunes or other apps. There are several ways to work around this:

• You can download normally on your desktop computer, saving the files to iTunes. Then, you can sync your iOS device directly to your computer, or sync your iTunes content using an iCloud account.
• There are many third-party apps which allow you to download files from websites into the app's own file manager for easy retrieval and playback.

Android

Files are always downloaded to the same location, which is a folder usually called "Downloads" (this may vary slightly depending on what browser is used (Chrome, Firefox, etc)). Chrome uses a system app called "Downloads" where files can be accessed at any time. Firefox and some other browsers store downloaded files within a "Downloads" folder in the browser itself.

Recently-downloaded files can be accessed from the Notification bar; swiping down will show the downloaded files as a new "card", which you tap on to open. Opening a file depends on what apps are installed on the Android device. Audio files are opened in the device's default audio app. If a file type does not have a default app assigned to it, the Android system alerts the user.

CONTENTS

Pianists on the recordings: [1]Brendan Fox, [2]Ruben Piirainen

The price of this publication includes access to companion recorded piano accompaniments online,
for download or streaming, using the unique code found on the title page.
Visit **www.halleonard.com/mylibrary** and enter the access code.

Arabian Dance
("Coffee")

Pyotr Il'yich Tchaikovsky

Allegretto (♪ = 80)

Trumpet in B♭

Piano

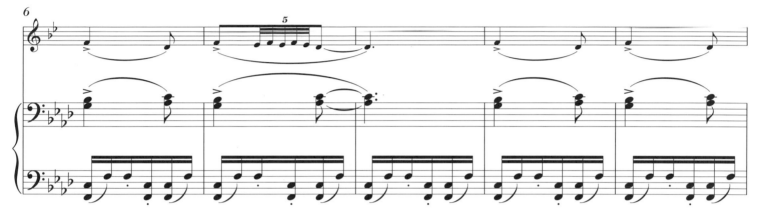

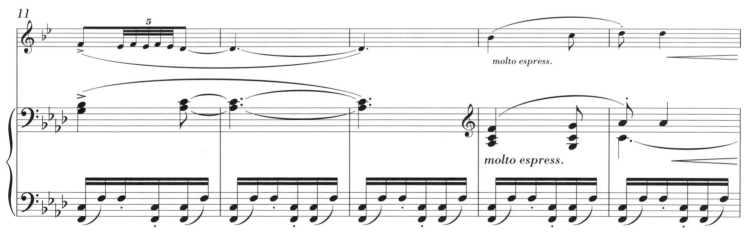

Chinese Dance
("Tea")

Pyotr Il'yich Tchaikovsky

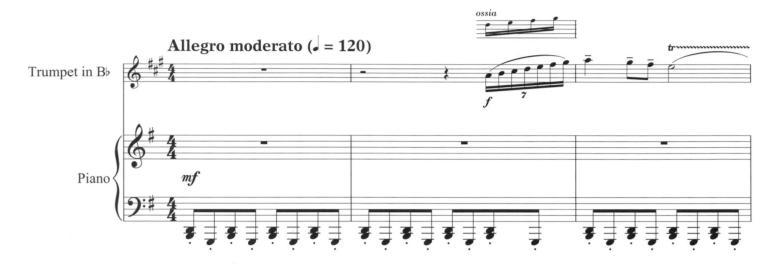

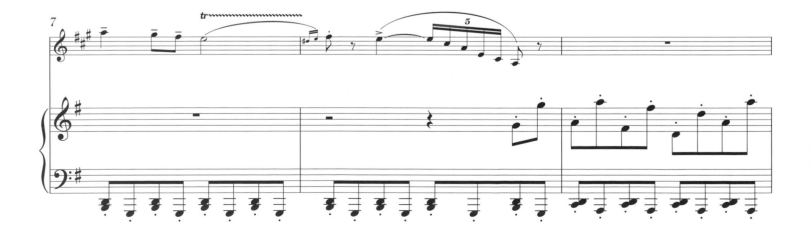

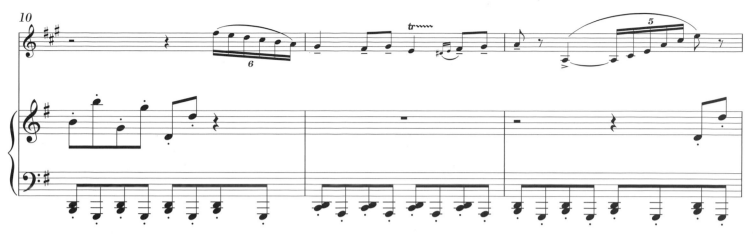

Dance of the Reed Flutes

Pyotr Il'yich Tchaikovsky

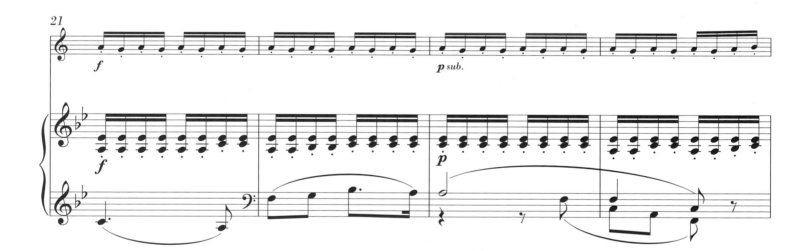

Dance of the Sugar Plum Fairy

Pyotr Il'yich Tchaikovsky

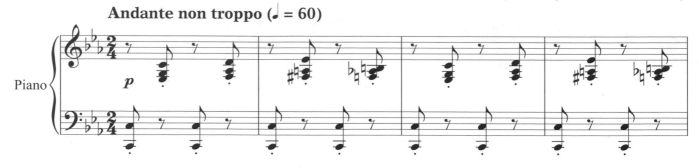

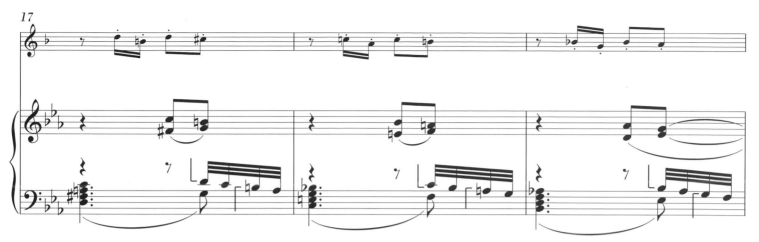

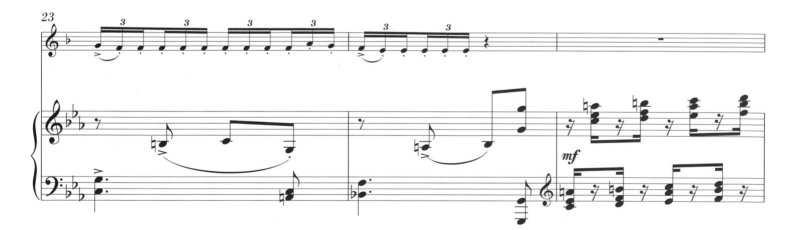

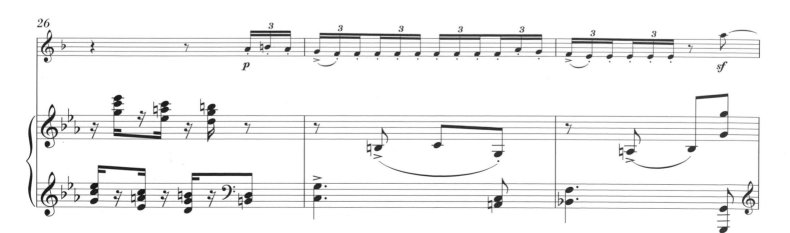

March

Pyotr Il'yich Tchaikovsky

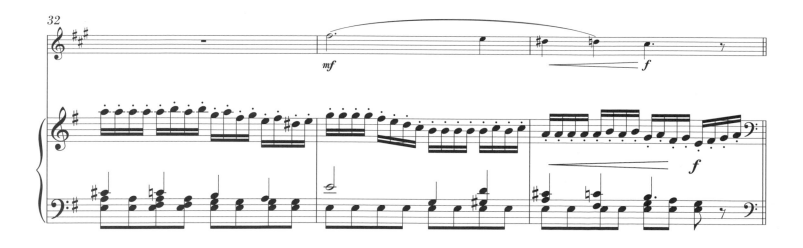

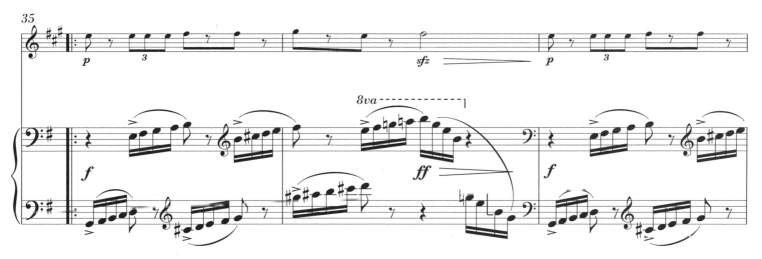

* The player may choose to omit these notes.

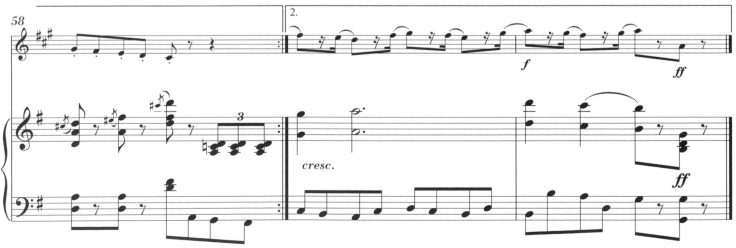

* The player may choose to omit these notes.

This page has been intentionally left blank to facilitate page turns.

Miniature Overture

Pyotr Il'yich Tchaikovsky

* The player may choose to omit these notes.

* The player may choose to omit these notes.

* The player may choose to omit these notes.

Pas de deux

Andante Maestoso (♩ = 50)

Pyotr Il'yich Tchaikovsky

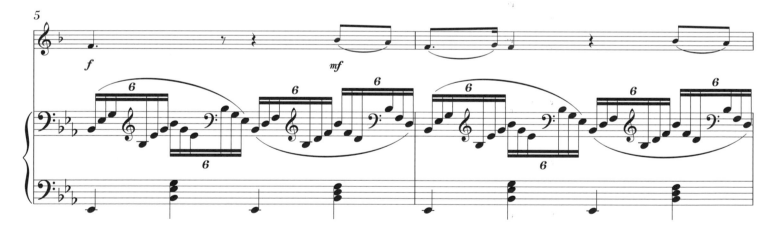

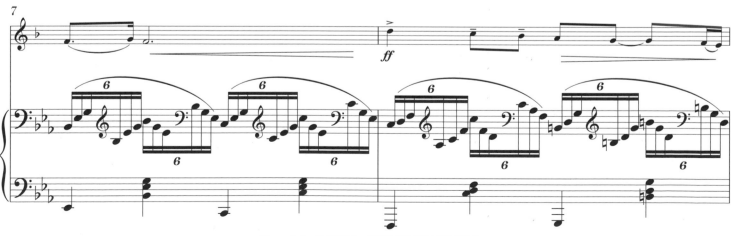

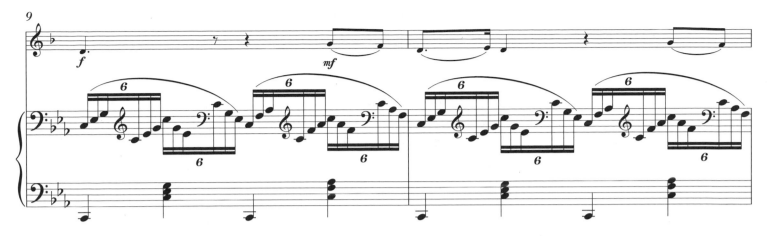

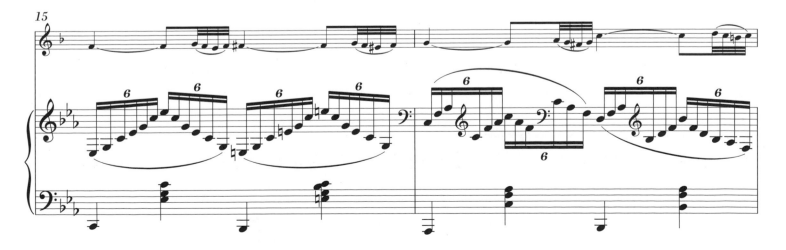

Poco più mosso

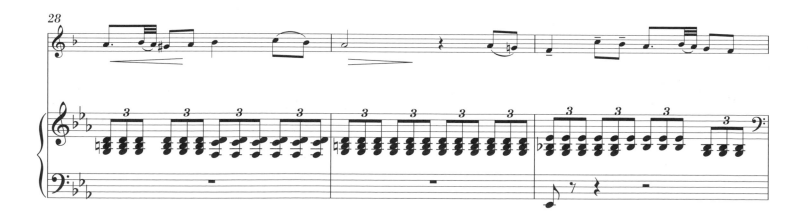

Tempo I

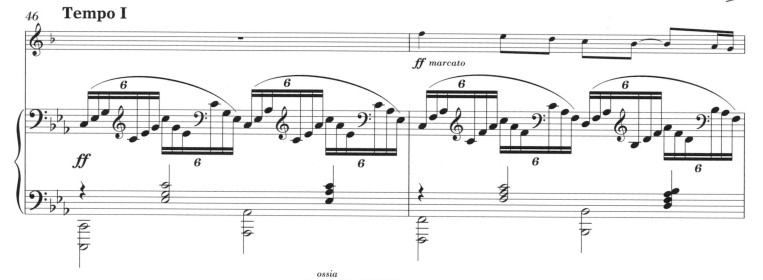

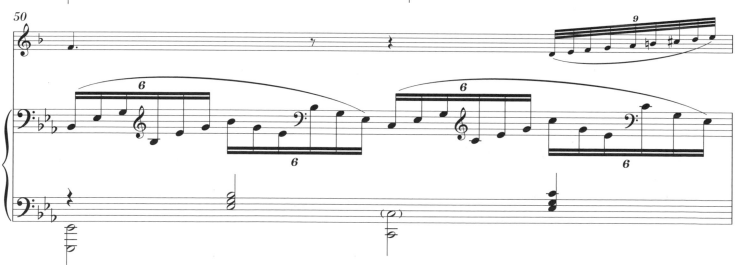

* The player may choose to omit these notes.

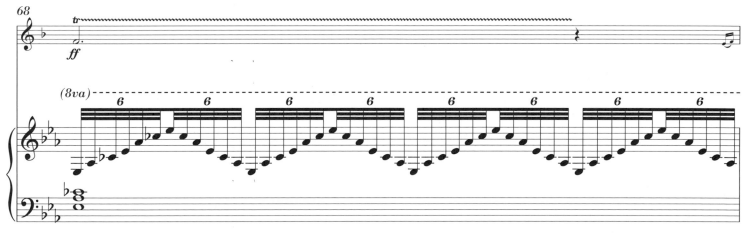

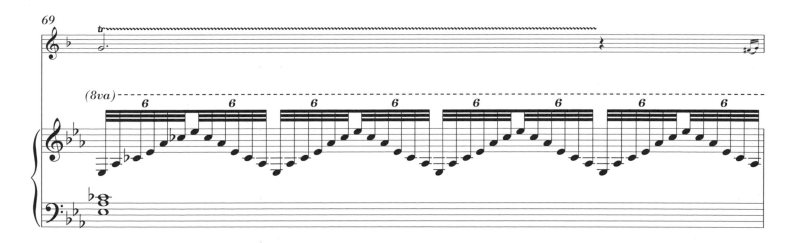

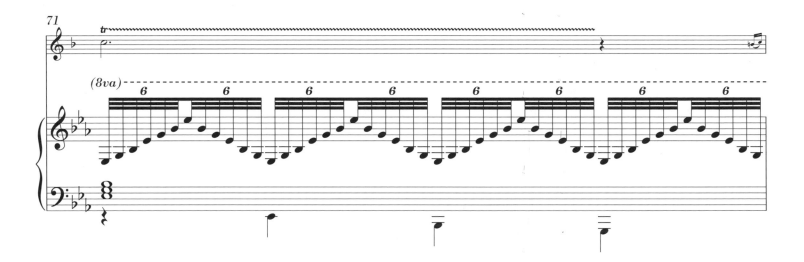

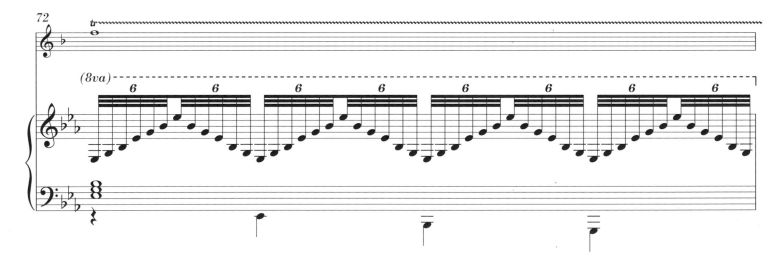

Russian Dance
("Trepak")

Pyotr Il'yich Tchaikovsky

Prestissimo

Spanish Dance
("Chocolate")

Pyotr Il'yich Tchaikovsky

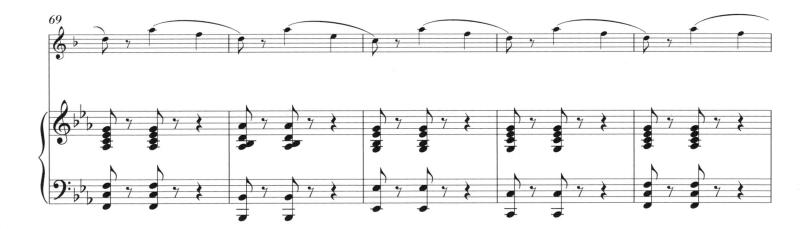

Waltz of the Flowers

Pyotr Il'yich Tchaikovsky

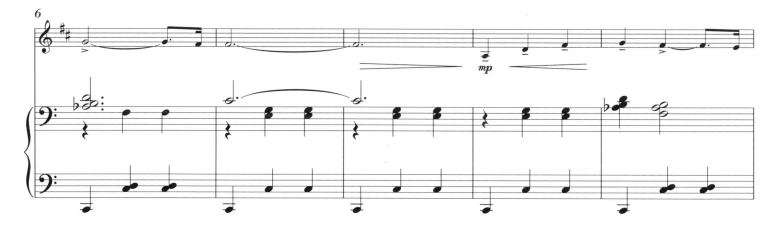

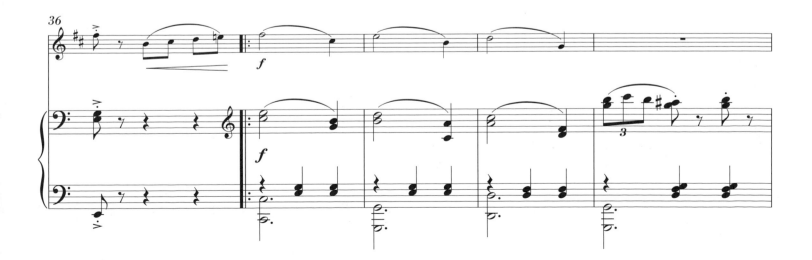

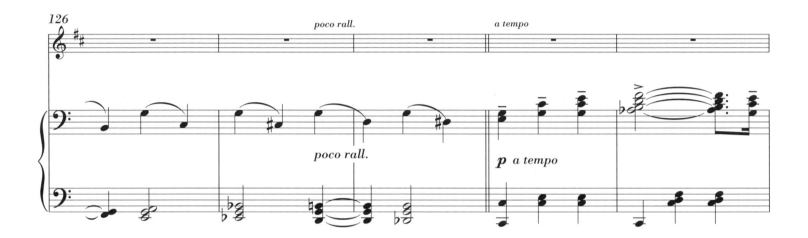

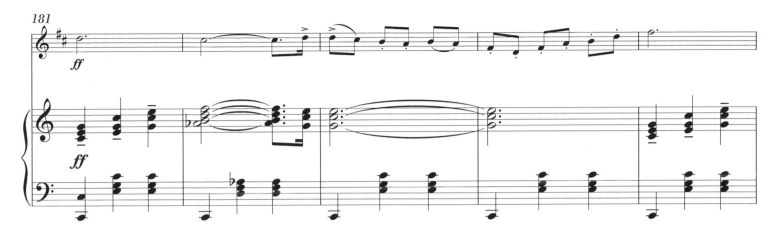